HANDS OF TIME

A BOOK OF POEMS

HANDS OF TIME

A BOOK OF POEMS

By

Pat Bordner

ISBN: 1-58721-695-7

1stBook – rev. 7/17/00

About the Book

A special gift of a clock triggered the idea for my book the "Hands of Time." Listening to the old clock steadily ticking on, measuring the minutes and hours. I soon began to see how much of life's moments are guided and directed by the hands of time. So as I live my life and the clock ticks on, I share in my book some of my childhood memories, places in time, people I encountered, and reflective times.

ACKNOWLEDGMENTS

I would like to thank the International Library of Poetry, for reading and editing my poems. Also, for the many opportunities and encouragement offered, that has helped me grow as a poet. Especially for the nomination to the International Society of Poets and election to the International Poetry Hall of Fame.

I also, express my gratitude to the International Society of Poets, for the informative symposium, you conducted in Washington, D.C.

In memory of Ira Westreich, appreciation for recording my poems on the cassette <u>Visions</u>.

My gratitude to HILLTOP Records who brought my poems alive through music.

Dedicated to my father, who gave me the gift of a clock, and my husband, who encouraged me to write about it.

CONTENTS

PART FOUR - REFLECTIVE TIMES

INTRODUCTION

The idea for my book <u>Hands Of Time</u> began in 1990. Receiving a gift of an antique clock from my father, during the Christmas season. I sat down Christmas evening and wrote the poem <u>Christmas Through Time</u> (on the following page.)

I soon began to see how much our lives are influenced by time. So I began writing poems using time as my theme. Recalling various experiences and times of my life. In doing so, I hope my reader's will recall, some special moments of their own.

INTRODUCTION

CHRISTMAS THROUGH TIME

The 92 year old clock ticks faithfully on the mantle,
    chiming out Christmas joy
A family heirloom and gift of a father's love.
Truly, a measure of the past, present, and future.

The Christmas tree stands near the hearth,
    symbolizing family roots and life
Yet, as the needles drop slowly a reminder of aging and temporary existence.

Dinner is served and childhood memories are shared,
    packages unfold one by one
Faces reflecting the spirit of giving and the joy of being remembered.

Christmas day passes and the clock steadily ticks on,
    now chiming in the New Year
Bringing new hopes, adding more links to life's chain and more history to record.

FOREWORD

For all that read my poetry.
Count the beats of my heart.
Follow the rhythmic patterns
and times of my life.

Gather thoughts from my life
stories, memories, places in
time, people I encountered and
personal reflections.

Find, how much our lives mimic
one another, and exchange tales.
Poetry will then signify the
creation of a harmonious song.

PART ONE

CHILDHOOD MEMORIES AND TIMES

DISTRESSED DRESS

Grand I felt in my maroon
plaid dress.
I twirl around and let
the air lift the folds,
skipping off to school.

Busy as a bee, with school
lessons, I am interrupted
by the recess bell.
Hastily, I dash for the
playground slide.

Tap, tap, I climb the ladder.
Rip, rip, dress tearing as
I slide.
I cry, what a hullabaloo,
unmindful a nun appears.

Led to the convent, whir
goes a sewing machine,
my dress is mended.
Stitching in time, memories
of a kind nun.

HAPPY TRAILS

Cheerful was I over the prospect,
of getting new winter boots.
One of six children, being taken
shopping was always a treat.

Browsing around the shoe store,
several selections were made.
Trying the boots on, I found them
to large or small.

Disgruntled, I decided to give it
one last try.
Hidden by a display, I found some
real eye dazzlers.

Genuine Hopalong Cassidy boots,
after my favorite TV cowboy.
All black with white bullhorns,
and stars. Nifty!

Perfect fit, the boots were mine.
Proudly I wore them to school,
where they were an instant hit.
Walking me on many happy trails.

SLED MAGIC

Snowy winter night blowing and drifting.
Morning finds the neighborhood hill,
laden with snow, looking like a
fluffy white pillow.
Nature's artist painting a beautiful scene.
Drawing me outside for a sled ride.

Shaking my sled from the frozen snow.
I grab the wet rope and take it in tow.
Sled bumping behind me and boots
crunching as I go.
Passing snow fort builders along the way.
I'll save that event for another day.

Slowly trudging my way to the top.
Spotting sledders zooming downhill.
Pushing the sled off and hopping on.
Knowing the ride won't take long.
It all seems like yesterday, although the
memory was captured, a long time ago.

IMAGINARY TRIP

Classic Chevrolet Coupe, running boards
and all, was parked in our backyard.

Safe as could be for our imaginary trip.
The battery was removed and put indoors.

Planning a trip to the apple orchard, my
brother and I, tossed a basket into the car.

Off we went imitating sounds of the engine
and rotating the steering wheel many turns.

Screeching the brakes and coming to a stop,
it was AW Root Beer time.

Moving on we reached the orchard, it was
really our neighbors yard.

Filling our basket with many apples,
thanking our neighbor again and again.

Beginning our trip back home, already
wishing for Apple pie.

BUSHWHACKED

Recalled to mind was a pleasurable,
childhood memory, riding on the
running boards of dad's car.
Often, my brother and I stood by
the driveway, in readiness, watching
for a glimpse of dad's car.

Dad's car in sight, simultaneously,
with a jump and leap, we landed
on the running boards.
Places taken, my brother grabbing
the driver side, and I the passenger
side, near a line of bushes.

Underway, enjoyable was the ride.
Until, my head bumps against a bush.
Whack! My hair tangles in a branch.
Dad stops the car to untangle my
hair, provide a scarf, and save me,
from being bushwhacked again.

CHIPSYS

Chipsys! What could that mean?
A word invented by my brother and I,
for chipping in.
It meant pooling our money
on an any occasion shopping spree.

Talking on the way to the mall.
Planning ahead which stores we'd go.
Deciding and agreeing on just the right thing.
Making sure we could haul it home.

We were like faithful lumberjacks,
splitting a log.
The cut was even, right down the middle.
After all, this is the way it should be,
when you do chipsys.

CANDLE WAXED

Speaking of the time I borrowed
my brothers skis.
Be wary of a brother who offers
them without asking.

Notice his secret disappearance,
or retirement to his room.
Heed the candle wax fumes
seeping under his door.

Seizing the opportunity, skis
in tow, shiny and glistening.
Happy-go-lucky I climb the
neighborhood hill.

Tiptop, skis fastened I descend.
Slippery and glassy were the skis.
Zigzagging, bobbing, and reeling.
Trembling I begin to flounder.

Wiped out! Toppling, tumbling,
and sprawling out in the snow.
Falling for skis, a mischievous
brother, candle waxed.

HANDS ON EXPERIENCE

Clink, clank, rumbles the hand
driven printing press.
I was a female forerunner in
high school industrial arts.

Anxious to match my skills
against my male counterparts.
I prepare for a visit from
the district superintendent.

In view, I stand near the press,
grabbing the operators handle.
Surprise! Underside the handle
was gooey, gummy, printers ink.

Hand stuck fast, still composed,
I convey to the superintendent.
"Printing is so enjoyable, I can't
take my hands off it, for a minute."

Released from bondage with honor,
keeping the male code.
Thou shalt not squeal on your
fellow pranksters.

PARADE FLOAT

Root beer float, sounds scrumptious!
Only I mean another kind of float.
A float my classmates and I built,
for our high school homecoming parade.

We were like conquerors on a mission.
Appropriating funds from a sponsor,
for supplies, such as, napkins,
chicken wire, and nails.

Haggling with a farmer proved fruitful.
Granting us use of a hay wagon.
Marching us forward to the actual
float building phase.

Wrapping chicken wire around the
wagon edge, we anchored it.
For days, we stuffed holes with napkins.
Exhausted garnishing the top last.

Showy and grand the float was finished.
Joyful, we pulled it to a burial vault
storage company, for safekeeping.
Preserving our float and life's memory.

UMBRELLA TROUBLE

Elevator operator calling,
Anybody going down?
Umbrella tucked under my
arm, I scoot in.
Please step to the back.
Oh boy, it's packed!
Sure will be happy, to
reach the main floor.

Door opening, I step out,
glad to be on my way.
What now!
A man is following me.
Each step I take, he moves.
Trailing me through,
the revolving door,
out to the sidewalk.

Stopping quickly I ask,
Why are you stalking me?
Laughingly he says,
"Please remove your
umbrella handle, from my
suit coat pocket."
Umbrellas on elevators,
can cause you trouble.

PART TWO

PLACES IN TIME

HANDS OF TIME

Leisurely, I enter dad's repair room.
Placing me in the hands of time.
Antique clocks of many styles.
Spring, gears, and parts about.

Clocks bold that bong, bong.
Softer pieces that ping, ping.
Westminster chimes play a tune.
One that dares to call me cuckoo.

Faces with Arabic or Roman numerals.
Bordered by designs or flowers.
Pendulums swinging to and fro.
Ticking, clicking, and tapping.

Hands moving slowly measuring,
the minutes and hours.
Guiding my pace, life's moments.
Directed by the hands of time.

TREASURES OF TIME

Bell ringing, as I enter the antique shop.
The musty smell within its confines.
Picturing old homes and attics in my mind.
A feeling I am walking through time.

Exploring the past of peoples lives.
Fine china placed on cabinets and tables.
Toys designed to amuse children and tools
of workers from many trades.

Listening to the bell ring once more.
I leave returning to present times.
Wondering what treasures, will be kept,
for the old antique shop.

SKATERS ALL ABOARD

Crisp winter wind tugging at my coat,
slowly numbing my face.
The sun shining across the skating rink,
surrounded by banks of snow.
Songs playing over the loud speaker,
touching my very soul.
Voices of laughter all around the warming
house just ahead.
Long ago a railroad car, now put to bed.
Smoke rising out of its stack, welcoming
all to come in.
Door squeaking behind me, it's good to be
out of the cold.
Warming my hands by the old wood stove, now
seeing skaters, where passengers once rode.
If the conductor was to appear, he would
cry out loud and clear SKATERS ALL ABOARD.

SMALL TOWN NEWS

Small town newspaper facing the river.
Tugboats horns echoing from its banks.

The old brick building weathered and worn.
Yet, indoors bustling with activity.

Smells of printers ink filling the air.
Coffee cups steaming from desk tops.

Typewriters rat-a-tatting away,
accompanied by ringing telephones.

Machinery thumping steady as a heartbeat.
Newspapers dropping off a conveyor.

Reach for a copy and hold the life
of the town.

HONEYMOON TRAIL

Honeymooning was enchanting in the North woods.
Rich in history once the routeway of voyageurs
and fur traders.
Winding trail through a forest of pines,
spruce, and birch.
Tree branches snapping, from the movement
of deer and bear.
Fishing rewarding, our days catch with
lake trout, walleyes, and northern.

Cabin tucked back, with wood stacked outside,
for an evening fire.
All is quiet, except for the loons echoing
over the waters, piercing the silence.
The symphony of songbirds among the grasses.
Magnificient in beauty, an ideal land, for a
walk down honeymoon trail.

RESTORING THE PAST

Lighthouse standing on earth's edge.
You are the loneliest of sights.
Once piercing the darkness with
hand-lit glow.
Rotating prisms lighting the way,
guiding ships through the night.

Abandoned to the elements, along with
your evicted keeper.
Changing times have darkened your lights.
Restored you will shine again.
If only to mark the history of men.

FOREVER LEARNING

For old time sake, I visit the university
campus.
Familiar sights, bring back memories of
past times.
The walkways seem longer now.
The steps steeper and more countless
than before.
Buildings withstanding the test of time.
But, like myself much older.

Memories of studying until dawn.
Finishing, with diploma placed in hand.
Foolishly thinking, I had learned it all.
Years have passed, along with faded images
of teachers faces.
The world now my classroom and experience
as a teacher.
Knowing and realizing, the learning goes
endlessly on and on.

RIVER DWELLING

Little house near the river.
Standing on a hill, it's easy
to spot your chimney top.
Having stood through many seasons.
Your strength is measured by
forty years.

Winter days snug, warm, and cozy.
Spring, nestled in the pines,
birds trill away.
Summer sun brightens the rooms.
Fall colors splashed along the
river, resembling a quilt.

Cupboards tucked down low, with
a character all its own.
Signs of history, painting, and
carpentry work.
Loving care has brought you
through time.

LADY LIBERTY

Peaceful radiance of a beautiful morn.
The giantess stands on her tiny island,
over looking New York Harbor.
Carrying a torch for friendship, freedom, and hope.
Crown of seven spikes made for her head.
Representing many things, the seas,
continents, or even the sun.

Lady Liberty, symbol of freedom.
Your broken shackles and chains, can be
seen half hidden by your hem.
Yet, exposed across the desert sands.
For our liberated Kuwaiti friends.
May the joy of freedom shine across your land.
May the shackles be broken in other lands.

PEACE FLIGHT

Trumpets blaring from Bosnia,
sounding the anguish of war.
Summoning America for help.
Bosnia, America hears your call.

Our soldiers come resembling
geese in flight.
Come join our formation you
need not fly alone.

We will lift you on our wings.
Traveling together in trust.
Drawing strength and power
from one another.

Weary from a long journey of wars.
We will land with you for awhile.
Set on the task, of doing all we
can to restore peace.

When the season says, all is done.
We will take flight home.
Leaving the doves of peace,
resting on your hillsides.

PART THREE

PEOPLE OF THE TIMES

RIDE FOR PRIDE

Rounded cheeks like Santa Claus.
Robust was he, at 85, and full
of energy.

Known to tip his straw hat,
the old gent's bicycle was his
treasure.

Nothing special, just a pedal variety.
But, it gave him pride
and mobility.

Pedaling, to see his wife, at
the nursing home, was an
expression of loyalty.

Stopping at the bicycle shop, for an
adjustment or two. Helped keep his
dignity in tune.

Front basket making carrying
things possible and forever
storing his pride.

GOOD INTENTIONS

Jingle, jingle resounds the,
bakery door bells.
Signaling another customer,
had entered the store.

Curiously, I study an old woman,
at the counter.
Her face was weather-beaten and
her coat threadbare.

Order filled, she sits down,
near the window,
Hungrily devouring her rolls
with gusto.

Thinking she was needy, the
manager handed her a bag.
Ruffled, she threw it, catching
him on the forehead.

Although, his good intentions,
landed on the floor.
Better he was mistaken, than,
not caring at all.

HONOR GUARD

Old woman made her daily appearance,
at the road crossing.

Dressed warmly for the season her,
attire was old-fashioned.

Crossing the street much to slowly,
motorists beeped to hurry her on.

Many feared for her safety, but
pride insisted she walk alone.

Discreet boy meeting her at the
crossing, devised a way of helping.

Explaining his fear of crossing the
road. May I walk along?

Together, hand in hand they walked,
one young and one old.

Boy glancing back at his friend,
extending the school patrol flag.

RUN ON SANDALS

Pens moving and pages turning, all the students but one.
Hands idol bent in his seat, getting no work done.

A ragged white cloth covered his feet, gently I pull it away.
Despair poured from his heart and a tear rolled down his cheek.

Saying "shoes are out of my parent's reach."
Classmates mocking, sandals are for the beach.

Day gone by, I slide my sandals, on my feet.
Hoping to walk unkindness away.

Parading around for all to see, bragging of
their coolness and durability.

Each day less shoes are seen. Now a boy smiles,
because of a run on sandals.

OLD MAID

Judgment of my teacher was both
shallow and superficial.
I based my impressions solely on
her appearance.

White hair, buckteeth, and glasses
so thick, her eyes were distorted.
Resembling the bad card in a game
of Old Maid.

Voicing my disapproval of her
appearance, with the words adios,
bon voyage, and so long.
Convinced school was doomed.

"Give her a chance," urged my
mother. Reluctantly I agreed.
Gradually, it became evident, she
had qualities, I never expected.

Always patient and kind with a
real artistic flair.
She became a treasured friend,
thought of as the Queen of Hearts.

NUTTY PROFESSOR

Slipshod in appearance, my college
professor was dynamic and likeable.
Intense, lecturing energetically,
he was enthusiastic and exciting.

Approached by the raise of a hand,
an inquiry was made.
Will there be a quiz tomorrow?
Clearing his throat, he pointed
towards the door top.

Stating explicitly "no quiz, unless,
I drop papers through the transom."
Judging the shutter like door window,
height alone, convinced me a quiz
would be unlikely.

Next day, a shuffling noise, could
be heard outside the classroom.
My heart began to go pit-a-pat, as
the papers flew through the door.
Tossing in a lesson on assuming.

LOST IN THE SAND

What does a child know about
problems of old age?
Content playing in the sand.
I spot an old lady stepping
into the sandbox, congenial
she spreads out a rug.

Fascinated, I watch her create
the most marvelous sand cakes.
She had it all down to a system.
Fill the pail, tap the bottom,
and turn it over quickly.
Gladly, she shared her trade secrets.

Had I made a mockery or fool of
an old woman, leaving her
lost in the sand?
Maybe! I should have tried taking
her back, to a place or time, I am
not sure she remembered. Perplexed!

SPECIAL BOX

Looking for some perspective on
life, death, and history?
Visit an elderly person.
I had such an alliance with Sophie.

Fit as a fiddle, my neighbor Sophie
was in her ninetieth year.
Small in stature, she was spirited,
spunky, and capable.

Enjoyable were her stories of the
Depression era and school days.
On one occasion, she brought out
her special box, tied with string.

Trusted, I was handed the box
and permitted to open it-
Confiding in me, the soft pink
dress was for her burial.

Noticing the same sparkle in her eyes,
accompanied with pride,
perceiving her quiet dignity in
handling life's final details.

SHARECROPPER

Clenched, in my little brother's
hand, was a plum seed.
Determined was he, to plant
his own plum crop.

Chosen to help, I followed toting,
a shovel and sprinkling can.
Together we surveyed the yard,
for a perfect spot.

Planting by the front steps, each
day he checked for signs of growth.
Producing nothing, but a frown
on his face.

Slipping away to the basement,
I found the family plum crate.
Hoping to cheer him, I tied the
first of many plums on a stick.

Elated, picking plums, my little
sharecropper gave them away.
His season lasting, until, the
plum crate was emptied.

TRIBUTE TO AUDREY HEPBURN

Audrey Hepburn left the world,
making an indelible impression.
Forever, will she be remembered,
for her legacy of films, and
humanitarian deeds.

Truly, a goddess of the screen.
Possessing a regal grace, charm,
and photogenic beauty.
Appearing naturally wise, always
a vision of fashion.

Recalling her hunger, as a child,
she became an ambassador to UNICEF.
Offering hope and comfort to
the children of Third World
countries.

Farewell, the sun has come down.
Rest peacefully in your eternal
sleep.
For others will take care of,
your children.

PART FOUR

REFLECTIVE TIMES

MOON REFLECTIONS

Reflections over a nearby pond
The sky opens up with a full moon.

A soothing glow softening the very shape of things.
Calming the waters of troubled times.

Magical and romantic showing, who am I.
Erasing details overpowering, my mind.

Bouncing my ambitions hopes and plans.
Stepping into the moonlight, I dream my dreams.

PORCELAIN DREAM

Swinging open the cabinet door. I remove my
favorite doll.
Joanna, made of porcelain, wears an exquisite
red satin ball gown.
From the top of her dark coifed hair, woven
with flowers, she is a picture of high fashion.
Gently, I search for the key that winds her
concealed musical movement.
Turning it slowly, I hear the Blue Danube Waltz.

The music carries my mind to 19th Century Vienna.
Seeing well groomed horses pulling carriages.
Handsome men helping their companions to the
ballroom entrances.
Doors opening slightly and the music traveling
into the crisp air.
Catching a glimpse of dancers, swirling under
crystal chandeliers.
Spotting curtains of gold velvet and flowers
all around the bandstand.

The music stops. What a wonderful time, my
imagination had, with Johann Strauss' Waltz.

LIFE ON A LINE

March winds blowing, arranging my hair
in a most unusual style.
Kite tucked in hand, I climb the
bluffs of my hometown.
Hills where Indians once lives and roamed.

The houses seem miniature, down below.
Airborne the kite lifts higher and higher.
Soaring, gliding, drifting on and on.
Lifelike are the strings pulling and
tugging at my hand.

Reaching in my mind, and feeling life
through the line.
Wanting only smooth flying, but
experiencing some snags.
No matter, the pleasure of flying a
kite makes life worthwhile.

SEA BREEZE

Sailing with steady breeze,
capturing the wind.
Gliding smoothly through the
water, sails shaking in the wind.
Waves slightly choppy spraying
against the bow.
Beneath the blue skies, white
clouds floating by.

The wind touching my face,
thoughts coming to mind.
Relaxing to the rhythm of waves
hitting the hull.
Spotting a jagged line of trees ahead.
Reality awaits on the shoreline.

ORANGE BLIZZARD

Beginning with a sprinkling
orange drizzle.
Forest becoming a blizzard of swirling
orange and black monarch butterflies.
Hanging in clusters against a
canopy of cool green fir trees.

Butterflies hovering in billowing
orange clouds.
Light on your back and fluttering
in your face.
Dancing, flitting, and weaving.
Bold, dazzling, and hypnotic.

Flickering like a candles flame
in the shadows.
Silence falls, around the
orange snowflakes.
Broken only by the butterfly wings,
beating in the sunlight.

RAIN IMPRESSIONS

Rain gently tapping on the roof.
Beads of water sliding down the
windowpane, slowly slipping away.
Trees and flowers catching the spray.
Drops dripping into an empty bucket,
to be saved for another day.

People outside hurrying, umbrellas in
hand, dripping like ice cream cones.
Dog scratching at the front door
shaking its wet fur.
Windshield wipers squeaking back and
forth, composing their own tune.

Little boy sneaking outside, delighted
with a puddle dance.
Hearing birds singing harmoniously,
playing worm tug of war.
Chipmunk peeping out of his hole,
seeing nature replenished again.

WINTER CAMOUFLAGE

Gone are the leafy camouflaged of trees.
Standing stripped, being dusted by snow.
Storm roaring and snowflakes dancing
all around.
Sleet tapping at the windows and the
wind rattling the door.
Marshmallow rooftops clinging to the eaves.
Smoke rising from the chimney tops.

White drifts piled to the mailbox top.
Yards buried under a white blanket and
trees bend from the heavy snow.
Streets clean and white, untouched or
trampled by anyone's feet.
The magical white camouflage, invites many
with hats, coats, and mittens, come frolic
in the snow.

RUBBER BAND SURVIVAL

Trifling with a rubber band.
Stretching, snapping, plucking,
and strumming it.
Unaware of the articles value.

Insight into the commodity,
gained at a flying school.
Revealed through a demonstration,
in packing, a safety parachute.

Parachute lines spread across
the floor, folding begins.
Placing systematically at each
gather, a rubber band.

Rip cord pulled! Each rubber
band, designed to slip off, one
by one, regulating the tension,
opening the chute.

A rubber band survival, holding
life in the balance.
Similar to life, delicate,
fragile, and complex.

VOWS

Radiant, reverently the couple,
exchange marriage vows.
Hearing them recite in "sickness
and health," my mind strays.

Lost in thought, remembering my
grandfather, a inspiration model.
Faithfully loyal in caring for my
bedridden grandmother.

Drawing up a mental image, of him,
methodically braiding her hair.
Rummaging through a box of ribbons,
adorning her with pastel bows.

Recalling him carrying her outside,
and inadvertently forgetting her.
Panicky over the lapse, desiring
only she remain with him.

Refocused, listening to the words,
"I pronounce you husband and wife."
Time only revealing what challenges
the couple will face.

NEW YEAR THOUGHTS

Crackling fire warm and cozy.
The old mantle clock chimes
in the New Year.
Similar to one's birthday,
marking life's passage.

A notebook empty on the table.
Pondering over my dreams and
shining plans.
Until, real facts slowly fill
the pages.

Hope reaches through the
darkness of night.
Morning breaks, on a New Year,
with the possibility of change.
I wait with anticipation.

About the Author

Pat Bordner is a Commercial Insurance Rater and has a degree from the University of Minnesota. She is a lifetime member of the International Society of Poets and was elected to the International Poetry Hall of Fame. Currently, she has a display setup on the internet, (http://www.poets.com/Pat Bordner.html). She has been published in 45 anthologies, many by the International Library of Poetry. Pat has been featured on the Poetry Today show, WRTN 93.5 FM, broadcast from New York. She has received the Golden Poet Award in 1990, 1991, 1992. Also, the Editor's Choice Awards in '93, '94, '95, '96, '97, '98 (ILP). In 1999 she has been affiliated with HILLTOP Records, which produced three of her poems into songs. Released is the cassette album "America" and the CD "Let Freedom Ring." The CD, "Let Freedom Ring" was dedicated and produced for the troops in Kosovo. Pat enjoys writing poetry to create positive thinking and warm thoughts.